23	24	25	26	27	28	29	30	3
50.942 Vanadium	51.996 Chromium	54.938 Manganese	55.845 Iron	58.933 Cobalt	58.693 Nickel	63.546 Cooper	65.39 Zinc	
41 Nb 92.906 Niobium	42 Moly					47 Ag 107.87 Niobium	48 Cd 112.41 Niobium	4
73 Ta 180.95 Tantalum	74					79 Au 196.97 Gold	80 Hg 200.59 Mercury	8
105 Db	106					111 Uuu	112 Uub	

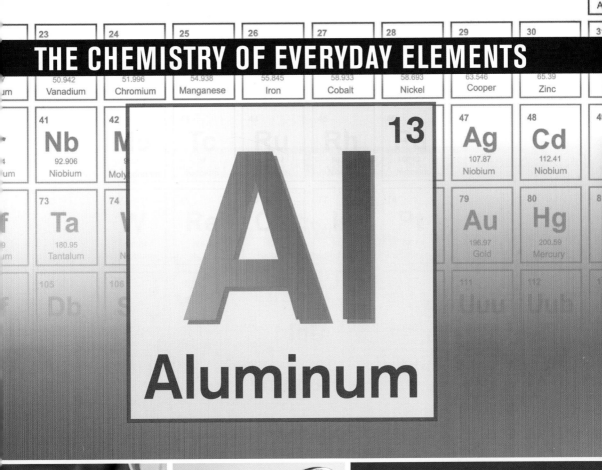

13

Al
Aluminum

Mason Crest

D1109251

THE CHEMISTRY OF EVERYDAY ELEMENTS

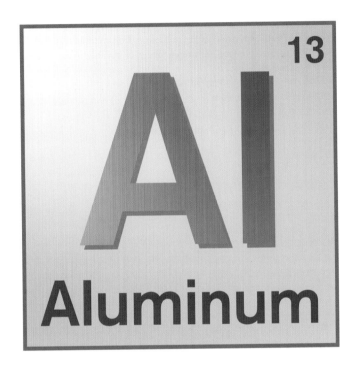

By John Csiszar

Mason Crest
450 Parkway Drive, Suite D
Broomall, PA 19008
www.masoncrest.com

© 2018 by Mason Crest, an imprint of National Highlights, Inc.

Printed and bound in the United States of America.

Series ISBN: 978-1-4222-3837-0
Hardback ISBN: 978-1-4222-3838-7
EBook ISBN: 978-1-4222-7943-4

First printing
1 3 5 7 9 8 6 4 2

Produced by Shoreline Publishing Group LLC
Santa Barbara, California
Editorial Director: James Buckley Jr.
Designer: Patty Kelley
www.shorelinepublishing.com

Library of Congress Cataloging-in-Publication Data on file with the Publisher.

Cover photographs by Dreamstime.com: Monkey Business Images (left); Selensergen (center); Hannade (right).

QR Codes disclaimer:

KEY ICONS TO LOOK FOR

 Words to Understand: These words with their easy-to-understand definitions will increase the reader's understanding of the text, while building vocabulary skills.

 Sidebars: This boxed material within the main text allows readers to build knowledge, gain insights, explore possibilities, and broaden their perspectives by weaving together additional information to provide realistic and holistic perspectives.

 Educational Videos: Readers can view videos by scanning our QR codes, providing them with additional educational content to supplement the text. Examples include news coverage, moments in history, speeches, iconic moments, and much more!

 Text-Dependent Questions: These questions send the reader back to the text for more careful attention to the evidence presented here.

 Research Projects: Readers are pointed toward areas of further inquiry connected to each chapter. Suggestions are provided for projects that encourage deeper research and analysis.

 Series Glossary of Key Terms: This back-of-the-book glossary contains terminology used throughout this series. Words found here increase the reader's ability to read and comprehend higher-level books and articles in this field.

A Useful and Versatile Element

Aluminum is one of the most versatile and surprising metals on the periodic table. It can exist at extremes yet remain common. It doesn't melt until it reaches 1,221°F (660°C), yet doesn't boil until an incredible 4,478°F (2470°C). Aluminum can be crushed simply by being stepped on but can be made strong enough to build airplanes and warships. It's a metal that is just about everywhere in the Earth's crust but that you'll never find by simply digging.

Aluminum is one of those metals that's all around you, all of the time, thanks both to the wonders of Mother Earth and the triumphs of modern science. In some ways, it's obvious; in others, you won't notice it at all. You probably don't see aluminum flecks in the soil while you're out for a walk, but be thankful they are there, since they are an essential part of modern American consumer culture. In fact, aluminum is likely an important part of your daily life. Do you have a smartphone next to you or in your pocket as you read this book? Are you drinking soda from a can? Did you ride in a car today? If so, you can thank aluminum for all of the silent work it does around you.

Aluminum is abundant, yet it can be hard to find. Unlike other metals such as gold, which can simply be mined and refined, aluminum essentially has to be created, or extracted from other compounds. While the Earth is generous with its aluminum supply, it took a roster of brilliant scientists—along with developments in other fields—before aluminum could be mass-produced at an affordable cost. For these and other reasons, aluminum is one of mankind's "newest" metals, only finding widespread use in the 20th century.

Beyond its obvious uses in our culture, this metal carries a bewildering array of characteristics that make it one of the most useful known metals. Take a soda can, for example. It feels very lightweight. (Imagine if they were still made of steel!) Aluminum's low weight-to-size ratio is one of its most useful attributes. The modern automobile and aviation industries, among many others, wouldn't be what they are today without this benefit of aluminum.

That same can demonstrates two additional traits of this marvelous metal. First, pick up your can by the top and bottom and lightly squeeze. Notice how the metal feels firm in your hands. Next, grab it by the middle and squeeze it lightly until it flexes. See how easily the metal bends? You've just discovered two of the other amazing properties of aluminum—strength and flexibility.

While aluminum's role in our biology is limited, there is a measurable amount of aluminum in your organs at this moment. In the lab, aluminum can trigger some awesome chemical reactions, if you're prepared with the right materials and safety gear. Someday, an aluminum reaction might be part of a hydrogen car.

These and other stories form part of the fascinating history of aluminum. However, to keep this production ongoing, we must be responsible with our efforts. While aluminum can be of great benefit, as with other metals, there are costs involved in its production. The financial cost of aluminum production tumbled rapidly after its discovery, but it still remains an energy-intensive process. Using those large amounts of energy has both financial and environmental impacts. Aluminum production also results in by-products that must be properly disposed of to prevent environmental damage. We can all play an important role in reducing the environmental and financial costs of aluminum production through one simple step: recycling.

Periodic Table

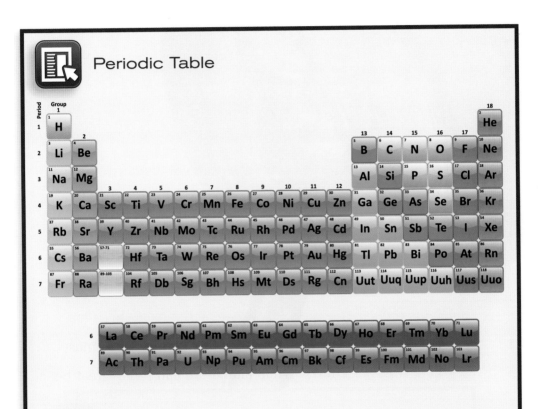

The Periodic Table of the Elements is arranged in numerical order. The number of each element is determined by the number of protons in its nucleus. The horizontal rows are called periods. The number of the elements increases across a period, from left to right. The vertical columns are called groups. Groups of elements share similar characteristics. The colors, which can vary depending on the way the creators design their version of the chart, also create related collections of elements, such as noble gases, metals, or nonmetals, among others.

Al ¹³
Aluminum

WORDS TO UNDERSTAND

alloys   metals made by combining two or more metal elements

electrolysis   breaking apart chemicals with the use of electricity

smelted   extracted ore from a mineral by heating or melting

Discovery and History

While aluminum is essentially never found in its pure and natural state, it is nonetheless found throughout the Earth. In fact, aluminum ranks as the most abundant metallic element on Earth, making up eight percent of the mass of the Earth's crust. Even including nonmetallic elements, aluminum is the third most common element found in Earth's crust (after oxygen and silicon). With all this aluminum, it might seem odd that there wasn't an "Aluminum Age" at some point in humanity's history. After all, the Gold Age saw gold **smelted** as long as 8,000 years ago; the Bronze Age saw the flourishing of copper, tin, and zinc 6,000 years ago; and silver and iron had their days about 3,000–4,000 years ago. So, why was there no Aluminum Age?

Al 13

Aluminum

The truth is that aluminum—of a kind—was used in ancient times. However, while the gold, silver and iron of the past civilizations were pretty much the same as they are today, the aluminum used by earlier civilizations was not the pure aluminum we use today. Instead, compounds that turned out to include aluminum were used every day.

Alum, which is a chemical compound, was used by Egyptians more than 5,000 years ago to help set dyes in fabric and other materials. Aluminum silicates were added to clay by Persian potters for added strength. A type of aluminum sulfate was used by ancient Greeks as an astringent. However, we don't find any true aluminum cups or weapons or tools in any ancient civilization.

The reason is that while the

Ancient pottery shows chemical signs of aluminum in the clay.

Earth has always had its aluminum—sometimes even in close proximity to the commonly used gold, silver, and iron—it wasn't actually discovered until relatively recently. Elemental aluminum was only discovered about 200 years ago, and it was only actually produced starting about 150 years ago!

Why wasn't it found earlier?

For such an omnipresent metal, it turns out that aluminum is quite stealthy. In fact, aluminum, in its pure form, doesn't exist naturally anywhere on Earth. All of the aluminum found on Earth is already bonded with other compounds and must be extracted and processed to be isolated as the element itself. While the ancients were able to make use of various aluminum compounds, it wasn't until the modern scientific era that we began to identify, extract, and produce pure aluminum.

We can thank a long chain of scientists for their pioneering work in this field: Sir Humphry Davy first identified the existence of a base metal that he called "aluminum" in 1808. Hans Christian Oersted used electro-chemical reactions to isolate aluminum from alum in 1825. German chemist Friedrich Wöhler is credited with isolating the first pure aluminum in 1827.

Later chemists and researchers found even better ways to produce aluminum. By 1856, French chemist Henri Etienne Sainte-Claire Deville used **electrolysis** to actually separate usable amounts of aluminum, beginning the modern age of aluminum production. (As a side note, Deville was funded by none other than Napoleon III, who, in addition to creating fancy tableware, was hoping to incorporate aluminum into his military armor.) By the 1880s, chemists Charles Martin Hall, an American, Paul L.T. Heroult, a Frenchman, and Karl Joseph Bayer, an Austrian, had perfected similar processes that are still used to this day to produce aluminum.

Many famous writers of the time took note of the rise of aluminum and helped popularize its growth. The French science fiction author Jules Verne wrote his famous *From the Earth to the Moon* about a space capsule made of aluminum, a material which no doubt added to the fantasy of actually flying to the Moon. Even famous British novelist Charles Dickens had this to say about the burgeoning aluminum industry: "Aluminum may probably send tin to the right about face, drive copper saucepans into penal servitude, and blow up German silver sky-high into nothing." And J.W. Richards, one of the first au-

thors to write about the aluminum industry, foretold the future when way back in the 1880s he wrote, "It has been well said that if the problem of aerial flight is ever to be solved, aluminum will be the chief agent in its solution."

The rocket created by writer Jules Verne in his famous science fiction story about a trip to the Moon was made of aluminum.

As with many historic discoveries, it took advances in another field to help the aluminum industry grow. One of the problems with the aluminum extraction process is that it requires large amounts of energy. In the early and mid-1800s, this was a problem. This is one of the reasons why Oersted—who first observed the connection between electricity and magnetism in 1820—had trouble producing more than small samples of aluminum in 1825. It took other inventors to come up with machines that could electrically separate aluminum from other metals. The mass production of electricity was also necessary, and didn't start happening until later in the 1800s.

The low price and durability of aluminum made it popular for household objects.

All this new technology created large amounts of this suddenly useful metal. The price tumbled from about $1,200 per kilogram in 1852, to $37 per kilogram in 1859, all the way down to $0.60 per kilogram in 1909. Even today, the price of aluminum is only about $1.59 per kilogram. Such a massive drop in price for such a versatile metal meant that it became affordable for manufacturers to buy and begin using it in commercial and consumer goods. The incredible diversity of aluminum uses continues to this day. Perhaps you could say that the "Aluminum Age" does exist, but that it began less than 200 years ago.

First Aluminum Products

During the latter half of the 1800s, when aluminum was a new, expensive metal, it was known for its shiny and lightweight qualities. Perhaps surprisingly, many ornamental objects of the period were actually produced out of aluminum, rather than being made of the more traditional "fancy" elements of gold and silver. Napoleon III, for example, offered aluminum cutlery for his most important guests, while others "made do" with utensils made out of the more common silver.

As the price of aluminum began to drop towards the end of the 19th century, early developers and inventors were finding ways to incorporate aluminum into larger consumer goods. The first passenger boat to use aluminum was produced in 1891, and lightweight railway cars with aluminum seats came out of J.P. Morgan's Hartford Railroad in 1894. Karl Benz, founder of Mercedes-Benz, exhibited a sports car made out of aluminum in 1899.

Al 13

Aluminum

While these early stage products in the late 19th century paved the way for the use of aluminum for transport, the first truly historic use of aluminum came courtesy of the Wright brothers, Orville and Wilbur, in 1903. In their efforts to become the first to successfully fly an airplane, they struggled to find an engine light enough to allow their plane to lift off the ground. An engine made out of aluminum, rather than the much heavier steel, proved to be the answer. Since aluminum is about one-third the mass of steel, the new engine developed for the Wright Brothers was a key factor contributing to the success of the world's first flight. Their pioneering ways announced the birth of an industry.

Without aluminum, would the Wright Brothers have been able to fly?

Wright Brothers
4-Cylinder Water-Cooled Vertical Engine

Bore	4 3/8 inches	HP	28 - 42
Stroke	4 inches	RPM	1325 - 1500
Displacement	240 cubic inches	Weight	160 - 180 pounds

Engine #17   Circa 1910

Soon after, aluminum **alloys** were used in planes for both World Wars, to be followed by development for use in commercial airliners. The supersonic jet Concorde, for example, made use of an aluminum skin, and the use of aluminum for airline

World War II airplanes

parts continues to this day. Aluminum also played an important role in space vehicles, from the first satellite—Sputnik—to the Apollo spacecraft, the Skylab space station, the Space Shuttle, and the International Space Station.

The Name Game

One of the most curious things about aluminum is that it is often called something else, depending on where you live. If you grew up in the United States, you used the word "aluminum" (ah-LOO-min-um). Throughout most of the rest of the world the metal is referred to as "aluminium" (al-you-MINN-ee-um). From a chemical standpoint, the

Al 13

Aluminum

How you pronounce the name of this metal depends on where you live.

international name makes sense—most elements in the periodic table end in "-ium" rather than just "-um," including titanium, potassium, sodium, magnesium and so on. This comes from the Latin origin of those words. In Latin, "-ium" is a suffix often used in nouns. (As an interesting historical footnote, it was Davy himself who also discovered and named potassium, sodium, and magnesium, thus making the term "aluminium" likely.) The International Union of Pure and Applied Chemistry (IUPAC), an international federation representing chemists across the globe, even made an official decision on using the term "aluminium" in 1990. However, the name "aluminum" has stuck in American society ever since the American Chemical Society adopted it in 1925, even in the face of international rejection. The element continues to live under these two names, with the US the lone holdover for the shorter version.

 Text-Dependent questions

1. Why wasn't there an "Aluminum Age," akin to the Bronze and Iron Ages, in ancient times?

2. What were the main financial and scientific triggers that helped popularize aluminum?

3. Provide the names of three scientists involved in the discovery and production of aluminum.

Research Project

Go to your local history museum—or find one online—and try to find pictures of historical aluminum pieces, such as the ones used by Napoleon III. Ask the curator or museum staff how the use of aluminum has changed throughout history, particularly in terms of decorative arts or displays. Note how ancient history displays will have few—if any—artifacts containing alum, but will have many made of silver, gold, or iron.

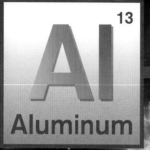

Al 13
Aluminum

Chemical Properties

The so-called "noble metals," like gold and silver, are found more or less in their pure state because they don't combine with other elements to form compounds. Pure aluminum samples, on the other hand, are almost impossible to unEarth. The reason is that aluminum in its native state is very chemically **reactive**, especially with oxygen. Any bare aluminum sample exposed to air will immediately grow an airtight layer, known as *corundum*, and the pure aluminum sample will be lost. Extremely rare native samples of aluminum can theoretically exist in what are known as extreme environments—or those with extremely low oxygen—such as the interiors of some volcanoes. However, for all practical purposes, aluminum is only found combined with one

or more other minerals. In fact, scientists have found more than 270 such ways that other elements can combine with aluminum.

Where Did It Come From?

Like many metals found on Earth, aluminum is created either in large stars or in the explosion of a supernova. Aluminum is created through the process of fusion, or the combining of atoms under immense pressure and temperature. The basic building blocks of aluminum are hydrogen and magnesium. Other types of fusion of hydrogen and helium produce heavier elements.

Extracting Aluminum

With its ability to oxidize or blend with other minerals, aluminum is nearly always found in **ore**. The ore that aluminum is produced from is typically bauxite, which is a clay-like rock resulting from the weathering of bedrock in tropic regions. Large bauxite deposits reside in countries such as Australia, Guinea, Jamaica, and Brazil.

The extraction process for aluminum begins when bauxite is mined from below the ground and sent to a grinder. Applying a hot solution of lime and caustic soda to the bauxite, also known as the Bayer process, extracts alumina, which is another name for aluminum oxide. This is a chemical compound of aluminum and oxygen. After being heated and dried, the alumina is ready to be refined.

Where there is bauxite, there is usually aluminum, so geologists look for this rock when searching for the element.

To transform this aluminum oxide into pure aluminum, the oxygen (the oxide part) must be taken out. This step, known as the Hall-Heroult process, requires three things: aluminum oxide, carbon, and electricity. Carbon **anodes** are placed into a molten mixture, along with the aluminum oxide, and electricity is applied to the mixture. Under this method, the oxygen within the aluminum oxide combines with the carbon anode, leaving only liquid aluminum. From there, the liquid aluminum can be formed into various sizes and shapes depending on what product is required. For example, some aluminum will be formed into bars or tubes, for

The Chemistry of Everyday Elements

products like ladders or bicycles. Aluminum can also be rolled into sheets to ultimately become aluminum foil, which can be as thin as 2/10,000th of an inch (0.006 mm).

Using Aluminum in Science?

Pure aluminum was first isolated in the science lab, thanks to the groundbreaking work of Davy, Oersted, and others, and it continues to be important in science today. Modern experiments with aluminum have unEarthed new, potentially breakthrough developments in a number of fields. Some of the most important advances being made include the production of advanced alloys. For example, in 2010, North Carolina State University professor Yuntian Zhu led a team that created an aluminum alloy as strong as steel. The alloy was created by adding some magnesium and zinc to aluminum and subjecting the compound to extreme pressure. The ability to mass-produce such an alloy could change some industries, thanks to the light weight, flexibility, and other characteristics

Inside a quantum computer

Aluminum is strong enough to be used in engine parts, such as these casts.

that aluminum provides as compared with steel.

The next step for aluminum could lie in the development of the quantum computer. A quantum computer harnesses the odd and powerful characteristics of the quantum (subatomic) world to solve problems that are simply not possible with current technology. For example, current computer language can only read zero or one; however, quantum computer bits, also known as quibits, can encode information as a zero, a one, or as *both at the same time*. This unusual quantum property, known as superposition, is still being researched by scientists. Currently, diamonds are the leading candidate for creating quibits. However, new studies are focused on using a much less expensive compound, aluminum nitride. As with so many other indus-

This amazing sculpture-like form is the result of molten aluminum being poured into a termite nest and then hardening.

tries, the inexpensive properties of aluminum could once again prove to be vital to the advancement of society.

While scientific studies of aluminum tend to concentrate on chemistry and physics, aluminum is used with great success in others fields as well. Entomologists, who study insects, and arachnologists, who study arachnids, such as spiders and scorpions—use aluminum in perhaps the most elegant manner. Since these small creatures (the spiders and bugs, not the scientists!) generally make homes below ground, it can be hard to study and visualize how they live. Ground-penetrating radar and other technologies help, but nothing beats having a three-dimensional picture of underground structures. To help study every nook and cranny of these creatures' complex worlds, scientists pour molten aluminum into abandoned nests. Once the metal cools and solidifies, what remains is a 3-D cast of the underground tunnel structure, which can be unearthed for hands-on research. Some of these casts look like works of art, with ragged branches extending in multiple directions.

Why Is Aluminum Important?

Aluminum is one of the most important elements on Earth because it is so flexible. This ability to bend and twist without losing strength or breaking makes it an excellent metal to blend with other materials. While aluminum is not strong on its own as steel is, it does have a very high strength-to-weight ratio because it is so light. When combined with heavier, stronger materials, aluminum can contribute to an alloy that is both strong *and* lightweight.

Many other natural characteristics of aluminum make it an attractive metal for industrial use, scientific research, and consumer products. Aluminum is **reflective**, heat-conducting, nonmagnetic, electrically conducting, nonsparking, and noncombustible. When processed

Aluminum

 ## What Makes Aluminum So Useful

Here's how aluminum's characteristics make it useful.

Reflective: Aluminum can reflect as much as 80 percent of incoming light. This makes the metal useful for mirrors and lighting fixtures.

Heat-Conducting: Aluminum conducts heat better than any common metal, with thermal conductivity three times as good as steel. This is valuable for making everything from cookware to car and airplane parts.

Nonsparking: Clearly, having a metal that doesn't spark can be useful in explosive or flammable environments; aluminum is often used in gas tank nozzles, for instance.

Nontoxic: Certain metals, such as copper, can be toxic to the human body. Aluminum's safety makes it essential for food-related products, such as utensils or soda cans.

Nonmagnetic: Since electricity and magnetism are two sides of the same coin, using a nonmagnetic metal is critical for applications such as electronic compasses, parabolic antennas, computer disks, and high-voltage hardware.

Electrically Conductive: The electrical conductivity of aluminum, coupled with its light weight and economic production process, make it a perfect metal for use in power transmission cables and the bases of electric bulbs. Aluminum only has about 62 percent of the conductivity of copper, but it is only a third as heavy. That gives it twice the overall conductivity for samples of similar weight.

Noncombustible: Since aluminum does not burn, except in the most extreme circumstances, it makes an excellent material for use in environments where fire could be an issue, such as in vehicles or buildings.

Corrosion-Resistant: Aluminum is so highly reactive with oxygen that it's actually corrosion-resistant. The oxidation that occurs when aluminum meets oxygen immediately forms a protective coating. On some metals such as iron, this coating is called rust and can be damaging, eating away at the metal under the rust. On aluminum, this coating does not spread beneath the surface and serves to protect the aluminum underneath. As a result, aluminum tends to have a long life, reducing both the need for maintenance and the environmental impact of replacement.

Al ¹³

Aluminum

as a consumer good, aluminum has an attractive appearance, is recyclable, and can be easily formed into a variety of shapes and sizes.

All of these characteristics help contribute to making aluminum a unique metal. While many other metals have some of the qualities of

The familar shiny surface of an aluminum can hides the elements' amazing traits.

aluminum, no other metal has such a diverse range of strengths.

With such a wide range of very useful traits, aluminum has become invaluable in both science and everyday life.

 Text-Dependent Questions

1. What is the name of the process used in modern times to produce aluminum?

2. List three of the unique characteristics of aluminum and explain how they differ from other metals.

3. How and where is aluminum typically found in today's world?

Research Project

Research the process by which aluminum is produced and create a poster board showing all of the critical steps. Include a map of where aluminum is commonly found and a flowchart diagramming the process from start to finish.

Aluminum and You

We've seen how useful aluminum can be in products and tools outside the human body; inside the human body, however, aluminum is something of a non-event. The human body typically does carry about 2/1000th ounces (65mg) of aluminum "onboard." That exists mostly in the brain, thyroid, liver, lungs, and kidneys. However, aluminum is not considered an essential element for human functioning, unlike metals such as zinc, copper, and manganese. And while aluminum for the most part is nontoxic, in excessive amounts it can cause problems.

Of course, it's easy to avoid ingesting aluminum, as it's rarely a choice on a menu. Or is it? In actuality, there are trace amounts of aluminum in some of the most basic human food items, like flour and baking powder. While you're unlikely to eat those powders straight, think about how many foods you eat that contain them, from cookies and bread to croissants and bagels. Aluminum compounds are also found in such common items as processed cheese, where it is used as an **emulsifier**, and table salt, in which it takes the form of an anti-caking agent.

As a result, the typical American adult ingests about a pinch of aluminum every day just from food.

How else does aluminum get into our bodies? The answer is, from nearly everywhere, but only in trace amounts. Every time you breathe, drink water, or come into contact with aluminum, from soda cans to aluminum foil, minute amounts of aluminum can enter your body. For the most part, this aluminum is harmless and passes right through your body as a waste product. However, concentrated exposure to aluminum can lead to health problems. For example, workers who deal with aluminum dust or fumes must wear masks or other preventive devices to protect their lungs. Some workers exposed to excessive amounts of aluminum have shown nervous system damage. Some research studies have noted a correlation between high levels of aluminum exposure and Alzheimer's disease, although nothing has yet been proven.

Overall, however, the U.S. Department of Health and Human Services considers aluminum to be safe. The Environmental Protection Agency (EPA), Food & Drug Administration (FDA), and Occupational Safety & Health Administration (OSHA) have set safe levels for drinking water, consumer products, and workplace air, respectively, and those limits are rarely violated. As long as you're not consciously ingesting large amounts of aluminum, it won't have an effect on your body.

Al ^{13}
Aluminum

WORDS TO UNDERSTAND

luster the way that an object reflects light, such as with a gentle sheen or soft glow or a more earthy look

oxidation the process of combining with oxygen, which often results in a change to the original material

Aluminum Combines

Aluminum has characteristics unlike any other single element on Earth. However, some of aluminum's greatest benefits—such as its light weight and bendability—can also be weaknesses. While pure aluminum can be formed more easily into shapes and is much lighter than steel, it is also much weaker. For heavy industrial applications, ranging from assembly-line machinery to airplanes, light weight is important, but durability and strength are even more so.

The way around this problem with aluminum is to combine it into an alloy. An alloy benefits from the light weight and flexibility of aluminum while gaining strength from the addition of more durable elements. Metals commonly used in aluminum

Aluminum

alloys include boron, copper, magnesium, tin, zinc, lithium, silicon, and manganese. Copper is mixed with aluminum if a manufacturer needs a lightweight metal that is also resistant to high heat, such as in certain parts of a car engine. For the transmission of electricity, such as from a power plant to a house, a copper-aluminum alloy could be used, but it would tend to be heavy; boron is a lighter-weight substitute for copper, and it still maintains a high level of electrical conductivity. Using boron in an aluminum alloy reduces the weight of the lines still further.

Scientifically designed aluminum alloys are extremely stable and can serve many modern industrial and consumer processes. But what happens when aluminum is subjected to chemical reactions? It turns out that in some instances, aluminum can be highly reactive. While some of these reactions make for fun lab demonstrations, others are more practical.

Chemistry and Aluminum

Like most elements, strange things can happen when aluminum reacts with other chemicals. From a real-world perspective, one of the

Aluminum can be used to remove the tarnish from sterling silver like these antique spoons.

most useful involves combining the chemical properties of aluminum along with baking soda and water to polish silver.

Silver tarnishes when it comes into contact with sulfur. The resulting compound, silver sulfide, is black, and as it clings to the silver it darkens it. You can polish silver back to its original **luster** in one of two ways. The traditional method, using polish, literally removes the outer layer of silver sulfide to unEarth the silver beneath. While this method is effective, it involves removing a bit of the underlying silver along with the silver sulfide. Over time, repeated polishing can result in the loss of a significant amount of silver. Since silver is a precious metal, most people would prefer to preserve it rather than rub it out of existence. The second way to polish silver is

After a bath in an aluminum solution, silver regains its amazing shine.

to let chemistry do the work for you. The main benefit of using a chemical reaction to clean your silver is that no silver is lost in the process; in fact, the silver sulfide is actually transformed back into silver. How does this work?

Sulfur tarnishes silver because the two elements bind together and form a simple compound, silver sulfide. While the attraction is strong, sulfur interacts even more strongly with certain other metals, including aluminum. Under the right chemical conditions, aluminum can naturally draw sulfur out of silver sulfide, leaving plain old silver behind, no buffing or polishing necessary!

The process is relatively simple. If you've got a sink, a large pan or dish, some aluminum foil, baking soda, and boiling water, you can do this yourself (under proper supervision). Place the tarnished silver on a piece of aluminum foil in the pan. Boil the water,

Cleaning silver with aluminum

mix in one cup of baking soda per one gallon of water, and completely immerse the silver and aluminum foil, making sure they are touching at all times. The silver sulfide will be attracted to the aluminum almost immediately, and lightly tarnished silver will be completely polished in a matter of several minutes. Essentially, what you are seeing is the sulfur being pulled out of the silver and onto the aluminum. The resulting compound—aluminum sulfide—will either stick to the aluminum or tumble down in pale yellow flakes. The combination of all these components—hot water, aluminum, baking soda and silver—generates a tiny electrical current that helps the chemical reaction. As a result, you may have to reheat the water and try again on more heavily tarnished pieces of silver.

In a Purdue lab, students worked on a method of using aluminum to get hydrogen.

Scientists are looking at the traits of aluminum to possibly power cars. More than a bit of aluminum foil might be needed, but scientists have devised a method to get hydrogen from the combination of water and an aluminum alloy. Purdue University engineer Jerry Woodall's process splits the hydrogen out from ordinary water when it is added to an aluminum-gallium alloy. The primary benefit of this process is that hydrogen is created on demand, rather than having to be transported or stored. This could play a critical role in the development of

An Aluminum Experiment

Under the supervision of your chemistry teacher, in a safely equipped lab, you can conduct an experiment that shows how Woodall's process uses aluminum to form hydrogen. However, unlike many other gases, hydrogen is extremely flammable, so this little experiment is strictly for the chemistry lab and adult supervision only.

The process of making your own hydrogen is actually fairly straightforward. As long as you can remove the layer of aluminum oxide on the outside of your aluminum sample, the pure aluminum underneath will react with water immediately. Oxygen will be pulled from the water to chemically react with the aluminum in an effort to re-form the aluminum oxide. When oxygen (O) is pulled from water (H_2O), only hydrogen remains. As long as the aluminum can remain in contact with the water, the reaction will continue.

To prevent aluminum oxide from forming, the aluminum must be in contact with another element. In Woodall's design, gallium does the trick. In this lab experiment, sodium hydroxide will work. Sodium hydroxide is the chemical used in many cleaning products, such as toilet bowl cleaner. To generate your hydrogen, pour some sodium hydroxide-powered cleanser into a glass bottle, then add some aluminum foil. Put a balloon over the top of the bottle and wait for the chemical reaction to occur. After a few moments, the balloon will begin to fill with gas—hydrogen gas. It's that simple! ***CAUTION: HYDROGEN GAS IS EXTREMELY FLAMMABLE. CONSULT WITH YOUR TEACHER ABOUT HOW TO SAFELY DISPOSE OF THE HYDROGEN IN THE BALLOON.***

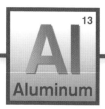
the hydrogen-powered car, as one of the greatest impediments to the development of a hydrogen car is the need to attach immense storage tanks to the vehicle.

The problem is tied to the reason why there isn't any natural aluminum in the world to begin with—**oxidation**. If you recall, aluminum reacts as soon as it encounters oxygen, forming a thin layer of aluminum oxide on its surface. While this chemical layer prevents

Aluminum could be used for parts of this hydrogen car, plus helping make its fuel.

any corrosion of the underlying aluminum, it also inhibits any further inter-action of the pure aluminum with the water. Woodall's gallium alloy helps, as gallium hinders the formation of the aluminum oxide, but it hasn't yet proven to be a complete solution.

 Text-Dependent Questions

1. How can you use aluminum to help remove silver tarnish? What is the process?

2. How can hydrogen be extracted using aluminum? Which molecule is the source of the hydrogen?

3. What is the atomic number for aluminum? What does an atomic number represent?

Research Project

Find other chemistry experiments you can perform that feature aluminum. Ask your science teacher for help once you have found some. ***Do not perform any experiments without adult supervision.***

Al ¹³
Aluminum

WORDS TO UNDERSTAND

chassis   the metal skeleton of a car or truck

crumple zones   sections of a chassis designed to collapse to reduce impact force

hydroelectric   power created by the force of moving water

wrought   made, formed, created. Note: wrought aluminum is used to describe aluminum alloys that are not cast directly but molded to a specific shape.

Aluminum in Our World

Most people are familiar with aluminum soda cans and aluminum foil, but aluminum is quite literally everywhere, from cars to planes to electrical wires. One of the most interesting characteristics of industrial and consumer aluminum is that it is rarely in the same form from product to product. Since aluminum forms alloys with other metals easily, manufacturers can tailor their alloys based on the strength, conductivity, or other characteristics they specifically need out of the alloy. In fact, there are so many alloys that a North American trade group, the Aluminum Association, Inc., created a system that lists more than 400 **wrought** aluminum and wrought aluminum alloys, along with more than 200 aluminum alloys. For example, aluminum alloys

Aluminum

that are "pure" aluminum (99 percent-plus) are assigned into Series 1, while alloys combined primarily with copper are in Series 2, and so on. Under this designation system, other common alloys include tin, silicon, magnesium, and zinc.

A Day in the Life of Aluminum

You wake up and hit your alarm clock, jump into the shower, and then brush your teeth. After getting dressed, you open the window, check yourself in the mirror, and walk upstairs. You open the dishwasher and take out a clean bowl and spoon for your cereal. After opening the front door, and the screen door behind it, you wait in the car for your ride to school. During the ride, you check your messages on your smartphone, and perhaps play a game.

In this scene, even though you didn't drink soda out of an aluminum can or unwrap leftovers covered by aluminum foil, you probably interacted with aluminum at least 10 times. Where were the possible aluminum interactions?

- your bed: aluminum alloy in the frame or rivets
- your alarm clock: aluminum parts in the motor, gears, or buttons

- your toothpaste: typically includes some form of aluminum

- your window: aluminum alloy in the frame

- your dishwasher: aluminum parts or circuitry in the motor

- your spoon: utensils often are an aluminum alloy

- your screen door: aluminum alloy

 Aluminum Alloys at Work in Our World

Here are some common examples where aluminum alloys are used:
- ground and overhead wires
- lawn chairs
- certain electric motors, like in dishwashers
- car bumpers, wheels, engines, radiators, and transmissions
- ladders
- window frames
- screen doors
- printing plates
- kitchen utensils
- airplane parts (right)
- telescope mirrors (coating)

Al ¹³

Aluminum

- your car: plenty of aluminum in the frame, wheels, engine, transmission, and other parts
- your smartphone: the screen is typically an aluminum-silicate blend, and the battery casing is usually aluminum
- your cell network: the wires and tower often have aluminum components

Depending on what your day is like, you'll figure to touch or even taste aluminum at numerous other times as well. Aluminum is found

People looking for stylish car parts often choose those made of aluminum.

in many consumer products that you probably use, from cosmetics to antiperspirants to antacids and even food.

The "Dark Side" of Aluminum

We've seen the amazing things that aluminum production has brought to the world, and how it's an important part of daily life across the globe. We've learned that aluminum is relatively cheap to produce and easy to recycle. But what are the human and environmental costs involved in the production of aluminum?

One of the negatives of extracting and producing aluminum is what's left over during the process. The residual product of bauxite mining is a substance known as "red mud." Bauxite ore, while containing aluminum, also consists of a mix of other particles and elements. For every ton of extracted alumina, between one-third and two tons of red mud is left behind. While the rock particles and salt in the red mud are not harmful, there are plenty of heavy metals and toxic substances that could cause problems. Red mud is stored in reservoirs and left to evaporate before it is buried. Certain harmful elements, like iron, which gives the mud its reddish hue, can leak into

Al 13
Aluminum

soil and groundwater. Some red mud is slightly radioactive, containing elements such as uranium. Even the liquid portion of the red mud can cause environmental problems, as the sodium hydroxide used to extract aluminum is highly toxic to both plants and animals and can cause burns in humans just through the inhalation of its vapor.

Aluminum refiners are well aware of these potential problems and do what they can to limit the environmental effects of the red mud. Some refiners use professional-strength presses and evaporators to dry the mud as much as possible before storing it.

A visit to a bauxite mine

Bauxite mining also requires a lot of energy—so much so that many of the biggest dams in the world have been created to primarily generate the massive amounts of electricity needed to run the mining sites. Part of the reason so much energy is required is the high melting point of aluminum. In order to extract the aluminum from the bauxite, extremely high temperatures are needed, requiring lots of energy. While dams are often thought of as "clean energy," they create environmental changes that can be problematic. When dams are built, land areas are necessarily flooded, as artificial lakes or reservoirs are needed to generate **hydroelectric** power. Flooded land typically means moving homes and people, who often have little or no say in the matter. Forests and wildlife are also affected, as flooded lands also mean flooded rainforests and habitat loss for living creatures. In addition, such dams can play havoc with the life cycle of fish, preventing some species from traveling to spawning areas.

This mine in Australia contributes to that country's huge bauxite industry.

Aluminum itself can present its own ecological problems. During the aluminum production process, collection areas called "catchments" often end up being saturated with aluminum. When concentrated in high enough doses, aluminum can be toxic to many animals, including birds and fish. It can disrupt many body processes, including kidney function and digestion. If not properly contained, concentrated aluminum can contaminate soil and waterways. When the polluted water evaporates, it can add to acid precipitation. If the concentrated aluminum is not enough to kill mammals, birds, and plants outright, it is stored and enters the food chain.

How can you help reduce the problems in aluminum production? The easiest step is to simply recycle. While recycling any metal is a good idea, it is particularly helpful when it comes to aluminum due to the vast amount of energy required to produce new aluminum. The sad truth is that even though recycling is more widespread than ever, more than 36 billion aluminum cans are still thrown away every year in the United States alone. How much aluminum is in 36 billion cans? Enough to rebuild every commercial plane in the U.S. four times over! While it may not seem like much, the simple act of tossing your soda

The strength and flexibility of aluminum has made it essential in carmaking.

cans in the recycling bin has a direct and dramatic effect on the world around you. How dramatic? Let's take a look at some other amazing facts about aluminum recycling.

Case Study: Use of Aluminum in Cars

While aluminum may show up in many products, sometimes it only plays a small role. In today's automobile industry, aluminum plays a critical role, in both form and function.

Aluminum matches perfectly with the requirements of motor vehicles, and its use has risen steadily over the past 40 years. Carmakers need a material that's strong and crash-resistant, and aluminum fits that bill. Aluminum can absorb twice the impact energy of steel, and its flexibility allows automakers to design accordion-like

crumple zones to further enhance safety. The light weight of aluminum helps cars have better acceleration, handling, and braking. Car doors made of aluminum can be thicker and more dent-resistant than those made out of steel while still remaining lighter. Plus, lighter body frames allow manufacturers to reduce the size and weight of other car components, such as the engine, since not as much power is needed to accelerate the car. On the outside, aluminum's brilliant shine makes it the perfect material for elegant trim, from dashboard accents to door handles and shifter knobs.

Moving forward, aluminum is going to play a large role in helping auto companies follow U.S. fuel efficiency regulations, which will require cars to average 54.5 miles (87.7 km) per gallon by 2025. An important way to increase fuel efficiency is to reduce weight. The Ford Motor Company, for example, is moving its F–150 pickup to an all-aluminum body frame. This will result in a weight savings of 700 pounds, or approximately 15 percent of the entire weight of the vehicle. That should greatly improve the pickup's fuel efficiency.

Aluminum is not just for mass-produced vehicles, either. Luxury automaker Ferrari has made a point of using aluminum in its gener-

Formula 1 race cars are carbon fiber outside, but aluminum inside.

al production cars, noting the safety and flexibility of the material. Moving up the auto food chain, aluminum also plays an important role in the **chassis** of Formula 1 (F1) race cars. Extremely expensive carbon fiber composites help them achieve supercar status. But F1 cars also rely on aluminum throughout their body structure, including between the layers of their carbon fiber skin. Aluminum alloys are also critical elements of F1 engines, thanks to their strength and heat tolerance.

Aluminum and Recycling

Many people associate recycling with trash. After all, even if you separate your trash from your recyclables, you still toss both away into big cans that get taken away by trucks, right? Maybe it's time for a new association with recycling: how about money?

Recycling has more to do with money than with trash. And

Al 13
Aluminum

aluminum cans, as it turns out, are the most valuable containers that you can recycle. Every can you turn into a recycling center is worth about one cent. That might not seem like much, but aluminum recyclers pay out more than $800 million every year for discarded aluminum cans. Perhaps as a result of these payments, Americans recycles more aluminum cans than any other consumer product every year.

The recycling of aluminum is a rapidly growing business and is helping the planet!

Few products are as recyclable repeatedly as those made with aluminum.

One of the reasons aluminum is such a good recyclable is that it can be recycled indefinitely. Unlike other materials, such as paper, aluminum does not weaken through the recycling process. The same piece of aluminum can be used over and over and over, and it will remain just as strong and flexible as it was in its first incarnation. Cans that are recycled can be turned from trash into fresh, clean containers in just 60 days. Due to these amazing characteristics, almost three-quarters of all the aluminum ever produced is *still in use today!* We're doing a great job saving energy and using our recycling bins!

The benefits of recycling all that aluminum are monumental. It takes 20 times the energy to produce a new aluminum can as it does to recycle one. In other words, you could make 20 recycled cans using the same energy it takes to make one new can. Recycling a single can saves enough energy to power your laptop for 11 hours. Each year, more than 60 billion cans are recycled, which saved 15 million barrels of oil. That's enough to fuel 1 million cars for an entire year!

Al ¹³

Aluminum

The good news is that recycle rates are the highest ever, but we can still do better. Americans toss almost $1 billion in aluminum cans into the trash every year, resulting in 1.5 million tons of recyclable waste making it to landfills. That's 1.5 million tons of aluminum that will have to be replaced through the extraction and refinement of new aluminum. The energy and environmental impact of all that production could have easily been avoided through the simple act of recycling. With a unified effort, we can work towards a world that enjoys the many benefits of aluminum without triggering environmental problems along the way.

Aluminum is not really used to make swords, but the element itself is a two-edged weapon. On one side are the enormous benefits from the products it

Glass and many forms of plastic can also be recycled, but not as efficiently as aluminum.

helps create. On the other are the hazards and costs created by producing aluminum. Balancing those two issues will play a big part in both our commercial and environmental future.

 Text-Dependent Questions

1. What are some of the most common ways you might interact with aluminum on a daily basis?

2. What are some of the environmental consequences of aluminum production?

3. How much more energy does it take to produce a new aluminum can rather than one from recycled materials?

Research Project

Start a recycling drive and collect as many aluminum cans as you can, whether through donations or scavenging. After counting them, take them to your local aluminum recycler (where you will be paid for your efforts). Calculate the number of hours you could power your laptop with the amount of energy you saved.

FIND OUT MORE

Books

Hasan, Heather. *Aluminum*. New York: Rosen Publishing Group, 2006. A brief look at aluminum, from extraction and refinement to its atomic structure and use in modern society.

Richards, Joseph William. *Aluminum: Its History, Occurrence, Properties, Metallurgy and Application, Including Its Alloys*. Kellock Roberston Press, 2008. A more complete, hard-science look at the physical and chemical properties of aluminum, along with metallurgy, mining and manufacturing.

Sheller, Mimi. *Aluminum Dreams: The Making of Light Modernity*. Cambridge, MA: The MIT Press, 2014. An accessible, general-interest reader about the impact of aluminum on 20th century society and beyond.

Websites

www.aluminum.org/aluminum-advantage/history-aluminum
The national advocate group for aluminum provides a brief, but thorough, overview of aluminum's storied history.

scifun.chem.wisc.edu/chemweek/aluminum/aluminum.html
scifun.chem.wisc.edu/homeexpts/tarnish.html
The chemistry department of the University of Wisconsin describes important and fun facts about aluminum, including chemical reactions and experiments.

www.hydro.com/en/About-aluminium/How-its-made/
Global aluminum supplier Norsk Hydro provides a detailed description of the life cycle of aluminum, from raw material to recycling.

SERIES GLOSSARY OF KEY TERMS

carbohydrates a group of organic compounds including sugars, starches, and fiber

conductivity the ability of a substance for heat or electricity to pass through it

inert unable to bond with other matter

ion an atom with an electrical charge due to the loss or gain of an electron

isotope an atom of a specific element that has a different number of neutrons; it has the same atomic number but a different mass

nuclear fission process by which a nucleus is split into smaller parts, releasing massive amounts of energy

nuclear fusion process by which two atomic nuclei combine to form a heavier element while releasing energy

organic compound a chemical compound in which one or more atoms of carbon are linked to atoms of other elements (most commonly hydrogen, oxygen, or nitrogen)

solubility the ability of a substance to dissolve in a liquid

spectrum the range of electromagnetic radiation with respect to its wavelength or frequency; can sometimes be observed by characteristic colors or light

INDEX

Photo Credits

Adobe Images: Dan Kosmayer 10, Barharlou 12, Goku 16, Bjorn Wylezich 25, Razvanmatei 27, Eugenesergeev 32, Rostislav Sedlacek 35, gjeerawut 36, David Pomborough 39, hanohiki 40, daniaphoto 46, superjoseph 49, afishman64 50, LightCooker 58, Denis Tabler 59, paylessimages 60. Antcastaustin.com: 28. Dreamstime.com: Yulia Grigoryeva 20, Warren Rosenberg 44, Krishnadas Chandreasekharan 53, Nataliya Hora 55, Chung Jin Mac 57. NASA: 22. Courtesy Purdue University: 42. Smithsonian Air & Space Museum: 15. Wikimedia: Armistej 18.

About the Author

John Csiszar is a freelance writer and article curator. After graduating from UCLA, Csiszar was a registered investment adviser for 19 years before becoming a writing and editing contractor. In addition to writing thousands of articles for online publications, including The Huffington Post, he has created, edited, and curated a variety of technology-oriented projects, from web pages and social media text to software help manuals. Csiszar lives in Hermosa Beach, California.